Holiday

WITH MATTHEW MEAD

create • decorate • celebrate

40

72

122

Holiday
WITH MATTHEW MEAD

TIME HOME ENTERTAINMENT

Publisher Richard Fraiman

Vice President, Business Development & Strategy Steven Sandonato

Executive Director, Marketing Services Carol Pittard

Executive Director, Retail & Special Sales Tom Mifsud

Executive Director, New Product Development Peter Harper

Editorial Director Stephen Koepp

Director, Bookazine Development & Marketing Laura Adam

Publishing Director Joy Butts

Finance Director Glenn Buonocore

Associate Director, Marketing and Communications Malati Chavali

Assistant General Counsel Helen Wan

Design & Prepress Manager Anne-Michelle Gallero

Brand Manager Nina Fleishman

Associate Production Manager Kimberly Marshall

SPECIAL THANKS TO

Christine Austin, Jeremy Biloon, Jim Childs, Susan Chodakiewicz, Rose Cirrincione, Jacqueline Fitzgerald, Carrie Hertan, Christine Font, Lauren Hall, Suzanne Janso, Malena Jones, Mona Li, Robert Marasco, Kimberly Marshall, Amy Migliaccio, Nina Mistry, Dave Rozzelle, Ilene Schreider, Adriana Tierno, Alex Voznesenskiy, Vanessa Wu

HOLIDAY WITH MATTHEW MEAD

Founder, Creative Director, Editor in Chief Matthew Mead

Managing Editor Jennifer Mead

Executive Editor Linda MacDonald

Senior Writer Sarah Egge

Contributing Lifestyle Editor Stephanie Nielson

Art Director Doug Turshen

Graphic Designer David Huang

Studio Assistants/Designers Lisa Bisson and Lisa Smith-Renauld

SPECIAL THANKS TO

Amy Locurto, Amy Powers, Kate Riley, Stefanie Schiada, Kate Wheeler

editor's letter

THIS HOLIDAY, Jenny and I will take our customary break when our daughters, Renee and Michelle, arrive to spend a few days with us. Our right hands at the studio, Lisa and Lisa, will also spend the days snuggled in with their loved ones.

To me, the holidays are all about family. I spend a lot of time preparing for special occasions with ribbons, wreaths, cookies, and sweets, but the season doesn't really come together until everyone is safe and happy and under one roof. That has been my approach with this magazine from its earliest days: It's a gathering place for talented people to share their ideas, recipes, and family traditions. From Utah, Stephanie Nielson offers darling paper ornaments you can make with your children. Stefanie Schiada invites us into her decorated Brooklyn limestone for a multi-generational Christmas breakfast. Los Angeles foodie Kate Weaver bakes up some of her award-winning cookies. Another talented California blogger, Centsational Girl Kate Riley, hosts a fab New Year's Eve Party. And from Dallas, Amy Locurto shows us how to package gifts easily and inexpensively for all the important people in your life. Join me in welcoming all of them to the pages of HOLIDAY. I know you'll make them feel at home, just as you've welcomed me for many seasons now.

I hope that this issue provides your family with new traditions, inspiring projects, and tempting treats for this joyful season together.

Merry Christmas and Happy Hanukkah,

CREATE

Brush the dust off that worktable: It's project time!
Take a tour of the house to gather up
supplies you already have on hand. Because shopping
is part of the season, head over to the crafts
store for some greeting card papers, wreath-making
materials, and sparkly ribbons. Lastly, tie on
your apron and try out some of these new cookie
recipes—they're sure to become part of your
holiday repertoire. With our simple instructions and the
advice of our favorite creative geniuses, these
projects will keep you as busy as those North Pole elves.

GREETING CARDS

Thanks to nifty scrapbooking tools called punches, you can make cards and tags that reflect your taste, fit your budget, and fulfill all your holiday gifting needs. Here are some ideas to get you started.

TAG, YOU'RE IT Gift tags are so easy to make, they're addictive. And they have many uses beyond just presents. Use them to label your holiday dinnerware storage, or hang 25 of them on a wreath to build an advent calendar. Simply choose papers and punches in a variety of shapes, and let your creativity take over. These tags (opposite) show how layering can make tags extra special. Adhere them using double-stick tape, and then personalize them using rub-on letter decals from the crafts store.

TREE TRIMMINGS To make a personal greeting card (this page), you'll need cardstock, which is heavyweight paper. For this card, trim the card stock to the size you want; a 5x14-inch piece of cardstock, when folded, makes a 5x7-inch card. For the front design, cut one smaller rectangle of patterned scrapbook paper, and adhere it with double-stick tape. Trace a tree-shape cookie cutter onto a second piece of patterned paper, cut around it using an X-ACTO knife, and attach it using more tape. Fold up the tree silhouette to reveal the pattern underneath.

YOUR PAPERS, PLEASE The most difficult aspect of creating gift tags and greeting cards is deciding which papers to use. There are easily thousands of colors and patterns to choose from, which a stroll down the scrapbooking aisle of the crafts or hobby store will show you. We settled on a lavender and turquoise theme (ABOVE). Matthew prefers to work with scrapbook papers because they have a sturdy weight, or heft, and are inexpensive. You can purchase them in 12x12-inch tablets or plastic-sealed stacks. Other tools include cardstock, hole punches, tinsel, rhinestone stickers, and decorative punches, such as this one. Simply insert paper and press, and it cuts the tag shape.

REFILLABLE SNOW GLOBE You can create this darling snowman card by downloading the template from HolidayWithMatthewMead.com and filling it in with your choice of different patterned papers. Tinsel bits, adhered with tiny amounts of hot glue, are twinkling snowflakes. Even if you decide to forgo the homemade card route, this is an eye-catching way to feature a special card you've received: Stand it up in a bed of artificial snow in a large clear-glass vase or candleholder, or under a cloche.

GIVE AND TAKE Use our downloadable patterns to make meaningful greetings, then highlight the ones you receive from loved ones. **1.** Trace an urn-shaped cookie cutter on cardstock, and use it as a gift tag. **2.** Cut leaves from different papers and form a poinsettia shape. For a card display, pin special cards around a foam cake round and set them on a cake stand. **3.** Layer a dove of peace over pretty paper backgrounds, and bend the patterned wings for extra dimension. **4.** Ornament shapes dangle from metallic cording affixed to the crease of folded cardstock. Glue the cording in place, then use a strand of tinsel to hide the cut ends.

TAKE A SHINE TO

Create a sparkling entryway display for greeting cards you give and receive. Prop a mirror on the hall table, and drape a piece of tinsel over it. Then hang cards from the garland using thin metallic twine. A platter corrals extra missives. You can download the templates for these card designs at HolidayWithMatthewMead.com, or turn to page 138.

HOLIDAY COOKIES

Once you sample the global flavors of these delectable delights from blogger Kate Wheeler at Savour-Fare.com, you'll want to make them part of your annual baking traditions

PRETTY ENOUGH TO EAT
One of the best assets of the Iced Ginger Cookies is their snap—or brittle, crispy consistency. Baked by Kate Wheeler of Savour-Fare.com, they stand up as edible ornaments and package decorations as well. Kate's 4-year-old daughter Madeleine declared them her favorite cookie of the afternoon baking session.

SEAL AND SHIP
Bake an extra batch of cookies to share. Use collectible tins lined with tissue paper or a linen tea towel to transport the fragile treats. Turn one cookie into a tag by printing a monogram, then affixing it to the cookie with extra royal icing. An icing snowflake, which you can buy where cake-decorating supplies are sold, decorates another tin of cookies.

A MIXED BAG The variety shown in these recipes (above) makes them perfect for sharing at cookie swaps or wrapping up in packages for the neighbors. "I aim for different textures. I want a platter of cookies that looks and tastes diverse," Kate says. "I like to include a spiced cookie, something with chocolate, something with peppermint, and a nut cookie." Every year, she makes her grandmother's Bourbon Balls, and something with cardamom for her husband, Kenyon Harbison. Their daughter Madeleine likes the pretty ones, such as these Cardamom-Black Pepper Trees with Juniper Icing (opposite). "I like to make them attractive, but I don't do full-on icing with every cookie," Kate says.

"For a lot of us, traditional Christmas cookies are influenced by other cultures."
— *Kate Wheeler*

Blogger Kate Wheeler's food passions go back to her earliest days making peanut butter sandwiches. "They were a revelation," she writes on her popular blog Savour-Fare.com. Though she opted for corporate law, and is now a full-time attorney in Los Angeles, she never ignored those yearnings to be in the kitchen, brewing up something tasty for dinner. Nowadays, dinner may only involve a ham sandwich, which is a meal her 4-year-old daughter Madeleine is stuck on, but it's going to be a *good* ham sandwich. "I know what it's like to be busy, to be harried, to feel like there are precious few hours in the day," she explains. "But I also know the value of a family dinner cooked from scratch, an afternoon spent rolling cookies, and a birthday cake baked with love." Nearly 20,000 visitors are paying attention to the simple, easy-to-prepare recipes she highlights, and her grandmother's Bourbon Balls made it to the Top 10 in the *L.A. Times* 2010 Holiday Cookie Bake-Off. Is all this attention enough to make her give up her day job? Not yet. But the time spent in the kitchen with Madeleine and her husband, Kenyon, is priceless.

AROUND THE WORLD When Matthew asked Kate (ABOVE, RIGHT) to come up with cookie recipes for this issue of HOLIDAY, she was in France at the time. She grew up traveling the world, and those experiences influence her food choices—even for holiday baking. "American cookies tend to be sweeter than European ones," she says. "But a lot of our Christmas cookies have European origins." To satisfy her husband's spice cravings, she chose tree cookies from Scandinavia. There are also samplings from England and France, as well as these Five-Spice Snails (ABOVE, LEFT), which use Chinese 5-spice powder—a combination of cinnamon, anise seed, star anise, ginger, and clove. Kate's grandmother's award-winning Bourbon Balls (OPPOSITE) are world-travelers themselves. "They ship really well, so I use them to send to far-away family and friends," she says.

"Now everyone expects Grandmother's Bourbon Balls, and I have to keep making them!" — *Kate Wheeler*

RICH ROOTS Thought to look like little gold bricks, these cake-like Almond Financiers (ABOVE) date back to the late 19th century. Kate makes her version using the recommended baking mold, which she bought at a local restaurant-supply store, but you could also use a mini-muffin tin. To elevate the look of these no-bake bar treats (OPPOSITE), Kate sprinkled on white nonpareils, pearlescent dragées, and icing snowflakes from the cake-decorating aisle of the crafts store. Underneath the decoration is Kate's take on crispy rice cereal treats. "There are only so many ways to make these," she says. She added a smooth, creamy layer of sumptuous, store-bought dulce de leche sauce.

DULCE DE LECHE CRISPY RICE CEREAL TREATS

These are a quick and easy no-bake Christmas treat. Dulce de leche can be found in most Latino markets, or you can make it at home from sweetened condensed milk.

You will need:

- 3 Tablespoons salted butter
- 1 10-ounce package marshmallows
- 6 cups crispy rice cereal
- 2 cups dulce de leche sauce, such as Nestlé®

1. Grease a 9X13-inch rectangular pan with butter.

2. In a large saucepan, combine the butter and marshmallows, and cook over low heat until the marshmallows are melted and the butter is incorporated. Immediately mix in the rice cereal.

3. Spread the cereal mixture into the prepared pan. Dollop large spoonfuls of dulce de leche sauce over the cereal mixture, then spread to cover.

4. Chill in the refrigerator, until the dulce de leche is firm, then cut into squares with a sharp knife. Decorate as desired.

CRANBERRY FLORENTINES

These cookies will be crispy if you eat them the same day you bake them, but chewy after that.

You will need:

> ½ cup heavy cream
>
> ½ cup granulated sugar
>
> 4 Tablespoons butter, divided
>
> 1 cup sliced almonds
>
> ½ cup dried cranberries
>
> 2 Tablespoons chopped candied orange peel (optional)
>
> ⅓ cup flour
>
> ¼ cup chocolate chips

1. Preheat the oven to 350 degrees.

2. In a saucepan, combine the cream, sugar, and 3 Tablespoons butter and bring to a boil. Add the almonds, cranberries, orange peel, and flour, and stir to combine.

3. Drop the cookies by the teaspoon at least 2 inches apart on a baking sheet lined with a silicone mat. These spread considerably during baking, so place them at least 3 inches apart.

4. Bake for 8 – 10 minutes, or until the edges of the cookies are brown and crisp. Let cool on the baking sheets for 5 minutes, then carefully remove to a wire rack.

5. Melt the chocolate chips with the remaining 1 Tablespoon butter in a microwave-safe bowl. Heat for 30 seconds, then at 10 second intervals, stirring between each interval, until the mixture is smooth. Drizzle the chocolate over the cooled cookies.

CARDAMOM-BLACK PEPPER TREES WITH JUNIPER ICING

Kate's husband, Kenyon, loves these cardamom-spiced cookies, which have the subtle, pleasant aroma of a fir tree, but taste sweet and crisp.

You will need:

> ¾ cup salted butter, softened
>
> 1 cup sugar
>
> 1 large egg
>
> 2 cups flour
>
> ½ teaspoon baking powder
>
> ½ teaspoon salt
>
> 1 Tablespoon cardamom
>
> ½ teaspoon freshly ground black pepper

1. Preheat the oven to 375 degrees.

2. Using a stand mixer on high speed, cream the butter with the sugar until fluffy and pale. Add the egg and mix thoroughly. Switch to low speed, and add the flour, baking powder, salt, cardamom, and pepper, and beat until everything is incorporated. Divide the dough in two, form into two flat disks, wrap in plastic, and chill overnight.

3. Roll the dough disks out to about ¼-inch thick. Using a tree-shaped cookie cutter, cut out the cookies and arrange them on a cookie sheet lined with a silicone mat. Bake the cookies until lightly golden, about 10 minutes, and let cool thoroughly before icing.

FOR THE ICING

You will need:

> ¾ cup half-and-half, divided
>
> 2 Tablespoons crushed dried juniper berries
>
> 1 pound confectioner's sugar
>
> Decorations, such as silver dragées and gold luster dust

1. Heat the half-and-half with the juniper berries to a low simmer, remove from the heat, and let the mixture cool in the refrigerator overnight.

2. Strain out the berries and combine the infused half-and-half with the remaining half-and-half and the sugar. Whisk together until a thick glaze forms. Brush the icing over the cookies, making sure to coat the sides as well as the tops. Let the icing harden.

3. To decorate, drizzle royal icing (see recipe, above) over the iced cookies, top with dragées, and, when the icing is firm, brush the trees with edible gold luster dust.

ALL THAT GLITTERS

Prepare to get your sparkle on as Linda MacDonald, author of the popular blog *Restyled Home*, shares easy-to-make glitter projects that reflect her home's signature holiday style.

ALL WRAPPED UP (THIS PAGE): A designated wrapping station is bedecked with projects Linda created for the holiday season. Set against a checkerboard backdrop of glittery 12x12-inch scrapbook paper — adhered using low-tack tape — the station is both pretty and functional. Linda then applied glittered trees to the empty spaces on the wall between each paper square. To make, first download and print the tree patterns at HolidayWithMatthewMead.com. Trace the patterns onto sheets of 12x12 glittered scrapbook paper. Cut out the shapes and apply hot glue to the back of the smaller tree and adhere it to the front of the larger tree.

SHOPPING LIST (OPPOSITE): Glittered ribbon has myriad uses during the holidays, beyond just dressing up packages. Purchase the glitter ribbon, scrapbook papers, and Zots™ glue dots at crafts stores, such as Michaels.

1 2
3 4

GLITTER AWAY **1.** Linda uses glitter liberally when crafting. In addition to creating new glitter projects each year, she repurposes outdated holiday décor with glitter in her favorite shades. **2.** Small vintage light bulbs are given new life and sparkle, again using Mod Podge® and glitter. Linda wrapped florist's wire around each bulb's base for easy hanging on a tree or to adorn a garland or wreath. **3.** Edible glitter is sprinkled on frosted cupcakes to provide sweet nourishment during busy craft sessions. **4.** Use a 12x12-inch glittery scrapbook paper as an impromptu place mat. Cut a 2x8-inch strip of the same paper to make a napkin holder for each place setting. Adhere the ends together using hot glue and wrap a narrow strip of glittered ribbon around the holder; secure using more hot glue.

ON A PEDESTAL
A tiered stand holds a tempting array of holiday treats and shimmering décor. Linda filled a collection of vintage glasses with candied almonds, and nestled cupcakes and cellophane-wrapped sweets on each tier. With her three children in-house, the treats won't last long. She hangs the glittered light bulbs from each level simply by bending the wire to form a hook that is used to secure each bulb into place. This garland effect adds sparkle and color to the display. Glittered trees (see templates on page 140) stand tall with the aid of small votives. Use Zots™ to secure the trees to the (unlit) votives. Linda likes to incorporate prettily wrapped gifts into her holiday décor. She wraps an assortment of hostess gifts and sets them below the stand for easy access when heading out to holiday gatherings.

"I love using glitter. It just makes me happy." — *Linda*

TREE OF LIGHT

"Not every tree has to be real," suggests Linda. Look beyond the walls of your home and adorn a window with shimmery candle decorations (this page). Using several colors of glittered scrapbook paper and the candle template found on our website, HolidayWithMatthewMead. com, cut out the patterns and adhere each piece in place with hot glue. Using clear tape, attach the candles to the window and apply them in a tree shape, spacing each tree about 1 to 2 inches apart. The result is an eye-catching holiday display that, combined with Linda's color palette, offers a break from tradition.

ALL THAT GLISTENS

Scrapbook-paper glitter pockets — filled with fresh greens, glittered light bulbs, and candy — hang in a trio on a wall (opposite), ready to be pressed into service as last-minute holiday gifts if needed. Linda dusted the greenery (artificial may also be used) with faux snow and tied on a pretty bow using the glitter ribbon left over from other projects. To make the pockets, follow the directions and use the template found on our website, HolidayWithMatthewMead. com. For a fun, take-away holiday party favor, fill with your guests' favorite sweets, ornaments, or small trinkets and hang from the backs of their chairs.

"Glitter casts a magic spell, instantly transforming the ordinary into something special." — *Linda*

1

2

3

4

1. GLITTERED CONE MEDALLION

Make in a variety of colors and hang in groups over your holiday table.

You will need:

- Cone template (found on our website)
- A stapler
- A sheet of heavy cardstock
- Glue gun
- Hot glue sticks
- 3 sheets of 12x12 glittered scrapbook paper
- A 1/16" hole punch
- Clear monofilament wire

1. Roll the cone template and secure using a stapler.

2. Cut a 3½-inch card stock circle.

3. Arrange the 13 cones on the circle and adhere using hot glue.

4. Cut a 2-inch and 1-inch circle from the glittered paper, and glue the smaller circle to the large. Apply hot glue to the back of the large circle and adhere to the center of the medallion.

5. Using a hole punch, create a small hole at the top of the medallion, string with clear monofilament line, and hang from a window frame or ceiling.

2. FESTIVE RIBBON CHAINS

Make this glittered ribbon version of childhood gum wrapper chains and use them to dress up glassware.

You will need:

- 4-inch x 1-inch lengths of glittered ribbon (as many as you need to create the desired length)
- Glue gun
- Hot glue sticks

1. Fold in half along the length of the ribbon.

2. Fold each end to the middle

3. Fold in half along the ribbon length again.

4. Fold entire ribbon in half.

5. Fold the ends in half towards the middle so that they meet.

6. Repeat with another length of ribbon.

7. Now with two links, fit the loop ends through one another.

8. Repeat the process, adding additional links until you reach the desired length of chain. Hot glue the ends together

9. Wrap each chain around a glass or votive.

3. SPARKLY RIBBON-WEAVE GIFTS

This elegant gift wrapping idea is pretty enough to make presents take center stage underneath a decorative table-top tree.

You will need:

- Plain colored gift wrap
- Several spools of glittered ribbon (measure lengths to fit each package)
- Glue gun
- Hot glue sticks

1. Wrap each package using the plain colored wrapping paper.

2. Beginning at the center, run a length of ribbon around the package and fold down the ends of the ribbon and glue the edges to the underside of the box using hot glue.

3. Using the pictured ribbon patterns as a guide, weave the other ribbons through each other, continuing to secure to the underside of the gift.

4. SHIMMERED-RIBBON CANDLE BOOKMARK

Make several to tuck into books for holiday gifts.

You will need:

- 18-inch length of 1-inch glittered ribbon
- Glue gun
- Hot glue sticks
- 3-inch length of narrow, glittered ribbon

1. Pleat and flatten the wider ribbon, securing each pleat with hot glue.

2. Make a V-snip at bottom of ribbon.

3. Hot glue each end of narrow ribbon to the top back of the candle to form the flame.

FUN FESTIVE WRAPPINGS

Using bits and pieces around the house, including the newspaper, you can make original, artistic gift packages and decorations. Let a pro show you how.

PRODUCED AND PHOTOGRAPHED BY AMY LOCURTO

FANCY DIY

"I guess you'd call this 'Fancy DIY,'" says Amy Locurto of the tabletop tree she fashioned one afternoon. Its red, white, and black color scheme inspired the gift tags and packages throughout these pages. Why black and white? Because of the newspaper strips she tore, twisted, and wrapped to make garlands for this tabletop tree. "First I tore all the greenery off an old topiary and spray-painted it black," she says. If you can't repurpose one yourself, look for grapevine topiary forms at the crafts store. Coil newspaper strips (Amy says it doesn't matter if the pages have colorful ads) around the tree from top to bottom. Tuck in artificial red berries, and place a star ornament to the top. The gift tag (opposite) is part of a package she's offering at PrintablesByAmy.com. Simply download her design, print it, trim, punch out the circle, and write the recipient's name.

Amy Locurto's mission is to have fun making crafts at home with her kids—using just what's around. "I don't really have time to make extra runs to the store," says the busy mom of two children, who also heads the corporate branding design firm Atomic Egg in Dallas, Texas. In addition, she publishes the popular blogs Living Locurto.com and IHeartFaces.com, and has an online store selling her printable cards and tags called PrintablesByAmy.com. Where does she find the time? "I don't sleep much!" she writes on LivingLocurto. com. "Seriously, I only get about five hours of shuteye a night!" It's this light-hearted approach to work that is at the core of Amy's success. "I'm a whimsical person, but I design large annual reports for a living, which are not as cute and crafty as my usual style," she says. So she started blogging when she realized that her creative outlet—sitting around the kitchen table making Star Wars® masks and fairy wings with her son and daughter—was something she could share with other mothers. "It took off from there," she says. So what if the dishes pile up in the sink? That's not something Amy worries about. "I hope what my kids remember about their childhood is how much fun we had," she says. Take a look at the pictures of blissful, partying children on her blog, and it's clear that's another thing she shouldn't worry about.

OF A THEME Once you round up the basic supplies and choose a color scheme, you can convey different looks for each gift, package, and decoration—as this display in Amy's Dallas living room shows (OPPOSITE). Amy (ABOVE, LEFT) relied on three main materials: newspaper, white banner paper from an office supply or The Container Store (ContainerStore.com), and fake red berries from an old wreath (you can also find stems of them in the floral aisle of the crafts store). For a hostess gift, Amy wrapped three pieces of zebra-print Duck® duct tape around a wine bottle (ABOVE), and hung on a monogram ornament.

HARDLY PLAIN PAPER PACKAGES These fancy wraps started as humble materials. The boxes are wrapped in sheets of inexpensive banner paper, which is sold on rolls. Amy uses for all sorts of crafts projects. "It's really thick, so it wraps nicely," she says. To dress up the boxes, she cut a wide band of the *Dallas Morning News*, added scraps of ribbon, and twisted rosettes out of more newspaper strips. As final embellishment, she raided her crafts leftovers for the doily, as well as the black twine that encircles the recycled paper envelope. To see how she wraps the rosettes, turn to page 137, or visit LivingLurcato.com.

BROWN BAGGING IT Printable labels perk up these plain gift bags (OPPOSITE). Amy added a ribbon band around the large bag, sticking it on with double-stick tape. Using scrapbooking punches, she cut a larger scallop-edge circle out of newspaper and a smaller circle label, which is available at PrintablesByAmy.com. Double-stick foam tape squares between layers give the tags dimension. For the small bag, she stuck on rhinestone stickers and cut a monogram tag using a scrapbooking punch from the crafts store.

"It doesn't have to be perfect. It just has to be fun."

NIFTY NOTIONS Let these ingenious ideas inspire you: **1.** Fill an extra picture frame with the graphic damask pattern of a vinyl wall stencil from the crafts or home decorating store. Made to peel and stick to your walls, the stencil adheres instead to the glass inside the frame. **2.** For a holiday display, print tags to spell out "JOY" and stick them to red ribbons using double-stick tape. Hang crystal drops from the ends of the ribbons, and stick the ribbons to the frame using Tacky Wax®. **3.** Ideal for a friend with a sweet tooth: Seal up a decorative treat in a clear cellophane bag from the crafts store. Print the label from PrintablesByAmy.com, then stick or staple it over the top of the bag. **4.** You can print Amy's designs as sticky labels, too.

"You'll find several packages of sticker paper on my office shelves," she says. For paper tags, she prefers printing on matte paper and recommends the 60-pound Polar paper from Red River Paper (RedRiverCatalog.com) as well as Staples® double-sided matte paper. **5.** Extra newspaper and artificial berries are easy-to-find materials. **6.** A fun teacher gift for your kids to make, fill mason jars with candy and print labels to stick on the lids or tape to the sides. **7.** Amy used a hole-punch to slip the label over festive paper straws her kids give to friends. **8.** To make this inventive rosette, twist narrow strips of newspaper and coil them tightly in a circle. Seal the end with hot-glue. Then, punch a scallop-edge circle and pleat one end to form a leaf shape.

A WEE HOLIDAY

Conjure some of your fondest childhood memories—or illustrate some recent ones you've enjoyed this year— by recreating scenes in miniature form.

PRODUCED AND PHOTOGRAPHED
BY AMY POWERS

LITTLE DELIGHTS
Trick out a tiny house (this one is a SnowyLaneCrafts.com kit) by adding paper awnings and pompom bushes (OPPOSITE). Make it sparkle with a thick coating of white crafts glue and a shower of glitter.

FAMILY MOMENTS
Look for unheralded plastic diorama-style ornaments at flea markets and thrift stores. Take off bits and pieces you don't like, and pose railroad model figures to recreate your family, as blogger Amy Powers did (THIS PAGE). Purchase the figures new at a hobby store and paint them, or buy painted vintage ones.

1

2

peace on earth.

Stretched out on her stomach, with her head propped on her hands underneath the lowest branches of the family's fragrant Christmas tree, young Amy Powers studied the tiny village her father set up each year. "It's my very favorite Christmas memory," she says. "He'd work through the night on it." More than just an assemblage of toys, Amy's father created hills and vales, a town skating pond, a tunnel, a downtown business district, and even an outlying farm. "With Perry Como playing on the turntable, I would watch this still, imaginary world under a sky of twinkling lights," she says. It's no wonder that's a fond memory for Amy, and why she is still drawn to miniature works of fantasy. As the blogger behind InspireCo.com and the publisher of Inspired Ideas, an online decorating magazine, Amy is known for her artful study of design and craft. Each year, she rekindles favorite holiday memories with tiny displays of holiday scenes. "There's something so magical about miniature worlds," she says. Often, her creations feature vintage collectibles, such as bottle brush trees and ornaments that she has inherited and collects. Never more than a few dollars at antiques stores and tag sales, the ornaments have the timeworn quality that suits her nostalgic vision and harken to those early seasons under the tree with "Have Yourself A Merry Little Christmas" in the air.

SMALL WONDERS Showcase vintage collectibles in charming arrangements. **1.** Amy Powers is no small thing in online publishing; she distributes a popular magazine, Inspired Ideas, and reaches a passionate audience via her website InspireCo.com. **2.** A wildlife scene perches on a porcelain cabinet knob, upended onto its flat surface. The pedestal is a watch face. **3.** Recreate one of the year's events, such as a vacation to France. "Make it a yearly tradition, and soon you'll have a lovely collection that is like a walk down memory lane," Amy says. **4.** A vintage ornament makes a hot-air balloon for a tiny passenger in a thimble basket. Use a jeweler's drill press or a metal punch to poke holes in the thimble. **5.** Plant a forest atop cupcakes using bottle brush trees glued to 1-inch mirror circles as bases. Decorate the trees with jewelry-making wire and beads from the crafts store. **6.** Turned over, a wine glass becomes in instant cloche. Stage a scene atop a round mirror coaster, using course salt for snow mounds.

3

4

5

6

MATTHEW

DECORATE

Go ahead! Daydream all you want about the happy
moments to come this season, with friends
and loved ones snuggled together in your home.
Cozy up your rooms with handmade adornments
and easy embellishments. Take inspiration
from what abounds in nature—from snow-dusted fields
to crackly pinecones. Gather up some of your
favorite collectibles to lace your rooms with memories.
Draw from a rainbow of bright hues to refresh
your decorating traditions. And when you sense
that itch to get started, just turn the page.

FRESH GREENS

Herald the season with inventive homemade wreaths featuring bright colors, interesting textures, and easy-to-find materials.

APPLE OF YOUR EYE

If your florist doesn't offer cut pieces of boxwood for this wreath, buy a small bush at the garden center, snip the branches you need, then plant the bush in the yard.

You will need:

- 2 bunches of boxwood and pieris japonica from the florist
- Floral wire
- 1 18-inch plain grapevine wreath
- 7 or 8 each Granny Smith and Golden Delicious apples
- 4-inch wood floral picks, with wires cut off

1. Cut snippets of greenery and form bouquets of about five stems. Wire them together at the base of the stems

2. Wire the bouquets to the wreath form in snug loops. Completely cover the wreath form in greenery.

3. Attach apples by inserting the ends of the floral picks into the apple, and then sticking the tips of the picks into the wreath, rotating the apples to show stems or shiny cheeks.

BOTANY 101 Matthew once arranged bouquets at a floral store, and he met his wife Jenny while working there. So, plying flowers and foliage is something he is practiced at—and something he enjoys showing others how to do. For the fresh takes on holiday greenery presented in these photos, he chose elements for their vivid colors, interesting textures, and varying foliage shapes. The holly leaves are shiny ovals, while the arborvitae snippets are lacy, for example. If they're not already in your yard, check the local florist or garden centers for these readily available cultivars (CLOCKWISE FROM TOP, RIGHT): holly, hydrangea, pieris japonica, cedar, arborvitae, and boxwood.

GIVE ME AN O!

"Ivy needs very little watering, so it's great to use in a live arrangement," Matthew says.

You will need:

- Several 12-inch long ivy tendrils
- 1 water pick from a florist or crafts store
- Salvaged wreath form, such as this letter "O" from an old sign
- Duct tape
- Clear monofilament line
- Satin ribbon

1. Put the cut ends of the ivy tendrils in the pick filled with water.

2. Tape the pick to the back of the wreath form using duct tape. Train ivy over the front of the form.

3. Hang the wreath using a loop of clear monofilament line, and tie a large satin ribbon bow at the top.

ZESTY LIME WREATH

With citrus in season this time of year, a sack of small key limes is an inexpensive way to embellish a plain wreath. These directions explain how to start from scratch with fresh greens, but you can also use the limes to enhance a pre-made wreath.

You will need:

> About 2 armloads of cedar branches, snipped from a nursery plant or backyard bush
>
> 12-inch wire wreath form
>
> 1 skein green floral wire
>
> 35 to 45 key limes

1. Trim cedar branches down to 5- to 7-inch lengths. If you have a lot of smaller lengths, too, you can wire together several stems into hand-size bunches.

2. Attach greenery lengths to the wreath form. Start with one piece, wire a loop around the stem, then around the form, then back to the stem. Lay another piece of greenery on top of the first piece, overlapping slightly to cover the wire. Repeat until the wreath form is covered in greens.

3. Cut a 7-inch length of wire. Push wire through a key lime. (You may need to poke a starter hole using a bamboo skewer first.) Wire the lime to a spot on the wreath, taking care to hide the wire under a bit of greenery. Repeat for as many limes as you like until the wreath is covered.

TRIMMING TIMELINE

One of Matthew's and Jenny's holiday traditions is making wreaths together. They divide the process into small, enjoyable tasks, such as hiking through the woods near his parents' New Hampshire home, looking for pine boughs to trim and fallen acorns to collect. Use their Christmas wreath-making calendar to start your own tradition:

NOVEMBER 23 - 30 Cut bits of greenery from evergreens, such as spruce, juniper, laurel, and white pine. Clip sparingly, so as not to damage trees or shrubs. If you purchase a tree or shrub for this purpose, plant and water the root ball before the soil freezes, according to instructions from the nursery.

DECEMBER 1- 10 Store the clipped materials in a cool, dry place, such as a basement or garage.

DECEMBER 10 - 12 Set up a worktable in the garage or on a porch that is stocked with supplies from the crafts store and floral supply center. To create multiple wreaths, you'll need several forms, ribbon, floral wire, floral picks, water picks, a hot-glue gun and glue sticks, and a spray bottle filled with water.

DECEMBER 10 - 16 Prepare your embellishments. Press the fallen leaves at the beginning of the week between pages of a phone book. Gather or purchase the seedpods, pinecones, flowers, ornaments, fruits, and nuts you plan to use.

DECEMBER 17 - 19 Assemble the wreaths. When completed, store them flat on the worktable, and mist them daily with water.

DECEMBER 20 Festoon your home, inside and out, with the wreaths. If you continue to mist them with water, they'll stay fresh through Christmas.

THE SPICE OF LIFE Variety is also the key to interesting holiday décor. **1.** Display the spectrum of green hues in ceramic vases (these are $2 to $5 flea-market finds) and cluster them on a tabletop. **2.** Bright hypericum berries pop against the dark holly leaves threaded into this birch-branch wreath. **3.** For dinner-party panache, wire greens and a hydrangea bloom to a 5-inch grapevine wreath, and it from a guest's chair. **4.** Myriad customizable wreath forms await in the garden center or crafts store. You can also repurpose forms from years past, or employ pliable branches and O-shape collectibles as wreath silhouettes.

LOOKING FOR ILLUMINATION

Cast a glow in the heart of a conversational grouping, such as a dinner table or coffee table, with this candle centerpiece.

You will need:

- Hot glue gun
- Hot glue sticks
- 2 8-ounce bags of chartreuse reindeer moss from the floral aisle of the crafts store
- 12-inch twig wreath form
- Salad plate or small platter large enough to hold the candles
- 3 pillar candles

1. Using hot glue, attach tufts of fluffy reindeer moss to twig wreath.

2. Place the plate in the center of the wreath, and arrange the candles on it.

3. Take care to extinguish the candles before they burn down close to the wreath.

"Wreaths are a traditional sign of hospitality, but they can look modern and new." — *Matthew*

WINTER WHITES

Transform your home into one of the season's prettiest scenes—a snow-covered landscape. Take inspiration from designer Tricia Foley's cottage retreat to blanket your rooms in cool serenity.

NO TWO ARE ALIKE

Just as each snowflake is unique, this pennant-style banner will vary with the materials you choose.

You will need:

- Die-cut paper snowflakes from the crafts store
- Double-stick tape
- 12x12-inch scrapbook paper
- Hole punch
- White twine

1. Tape snowflakes on top of patterned scrapbook paper.

2. Cut each piece of scrapbook paper into 3 pennant-style triangles, with short sides measuring 6 inches. (You will cut through the snowflakes.)

3. Punch holes in the corners of the pennant, and tie twine to join them into a garland.

HEAVENLY BUFFET

Who says the buffet has to be a standard rectangle or square? Set up tea and sweets on a round table covered in a matelassé bedspread. Candles add instant romance. For an elegant visual display, elevate a large cylinder vase or pot on a cake stand and fill it with floral foam, sand, or small pebbles that will anchor white-painted branches. Then string on ornaments and paper angels.

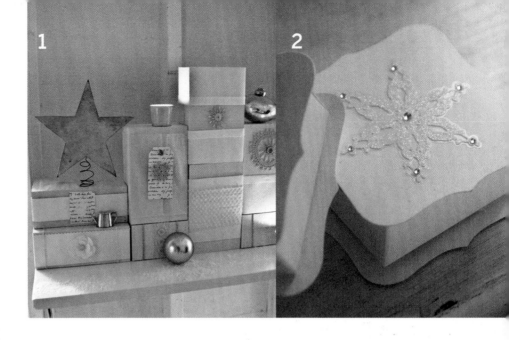

WRAPPING SPOT

Set up a pretty wrapping station (OPPOSITE) to ease your way through the holidays. A twig wreath sprayed lightly with white paint and affixed with a paper angel, marks the spot. Download the angel template at HolidayWithMatthewMead.com. A wood tote holds boxes and wrapped packages, a small wastebasket corrals papers, and goblets hold tags. Keep ribbons spooled by tucking them into canisters and trailing the ends out from under the lids. Even a teapot can hold twine or ribbon.

WAYS WITH WHITE

1. Stacks of boxes and tins labeled 1 through 25 are a sophisticated way to count down to the holiday.

2. Paper candy boxes, which are available in the candy-making aisle of the crafts store, become gift boxes with paper snowflakes and jeweled stickers.

3. On this side table, the base of a candlestick shows off attractive baubles, including embellished gift boxes and mini white ball ornaments.

4. To make this gift tag, look for card stock with old-fashioned script. Cut it into a tag shape, add a grommet at the top, and glue on a silver snowflake.

5. A one-of-a-kind ornament that's easy enough for children to make: Glue a white seashell to the center of a stiff card stock doily that is sold as a coaster.

6. To create an all-white look, gather items that you already have, such as dinnerware and linens. Then add a few inexpensive accessories, such as lanterns from an import store.

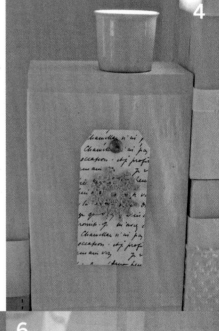

SEA STAR

The natural beauty of this seashell wreath is appealing year-round.

You will need:

Bulk seashells from the craft store or online shop, such as seashellworld.com

Hot glue gun

Hot glue sticks

10-inch straw wreath form

White spray paint

Silk leaves from the crafts store

1. Hot-glue seashells around the wreath form.

2. Spray it lightly with paint.

3. When dry, tie on sequined white leaves and hang.

SCENE STEALER
Whether it's cardboard star lights or a wreath formed out of seashells, the unifying white hue melds them into a wintry scene. This former chicken coop is designer Tricia Foley's backyard getaway through spring, summer, and fall. Come winter, flickering candles and layers of soft linens on the daybed warm the cozy space.

PACKAGING DETAILS

1. Look for interesting gift boxes, such as these cupcake-style ephemera. Add garnishes of twinkly glass beads glued to scrapbook-paper flowers.

2. The paper versions of Christmas stockings can be used as gift tags or as place cards on the table. Decorate them with scrapbooking stickers, such as these flowers and snowflakes. You can download the stocking templates at HolidayWithMatthewMead.com, or turn to page 142.

HOUSE ADORNMENTS

3. Jewelry-making supplies, such as these layered flowers, make quick ornaments or gift toppers. Paint them white and add a hanging string.

4. Feature a paper snowflake, backed by gauzy fabric or sheer paper, in a peek-a-boo window or in the single pane of a divided window.

TABLE SETTINGS

5. Gain more centerpiece impact by clustering glowing candles together. Group them on a round platter, plate, or tray, and fill in around the base with clear glass floral beads.

6. Paper flowers make pretty napkin rings. Glue them to a paper band and adorn the center with a rhinestone sticker (also from the scrapbooking supplies aisle at the crafts center).

PULL IT TOGETHER
When decking the halls white, choose baubles in a variety of similar hues, including pearl, clear, and metallic silver. Natural greenery, such as tabletop-size trees, fir branches, and fresh hydrangea blooms are at home in the snowy scene.

"Choosing a one-color scheme cuts down on extra clutter—everything you bring into your home will fit seamlessly." — *Matthew*

TAKE AWAY GIFTS
Personalize your own nativity or wintry
town for a charming tabletop vignette.
Look for small wooden buildings, such as
these mini-birdhouses, at crafts stores
and woodworking shops. Paint them white,
and then add paper ribbon snippets,
beads, and flowers to cover the holes.

PACKAGE ADORNMENT

Once a popular tree ornament, crochet snowflakes abound at flea markets and estate sales. Tie one on as a delicate package embellishment. If you prefer to make one yourself, it is considered an easy skill for beginners. Watch how-to videos on the internet (we offer a link to one by CrochetGeek at our website HolidayWithMatthewMead.com), or take a class at a local knitting or crafts store.

NATURAL HOLIDAY

Take advantage of the season's bounty—a fragrant supply of spices, berries, and fresh greens—to create easy decorating projects that will infuse your house with homespun warmth.

CORNUCOPIA OF IDEAS This time of year, it's a cinch to gather up natural offerings that are plentiful in the grocery store, and maybe even your own back yard. Pine trees shed their cones, the cranberry harvest hits the produce aisle, and ingredients for potpourri or mulled cider are set out in bulk bins. Dig in and fill your basket. Whether you just array items in a wooden platter (this page), or spend an afternoon fashioning them into fetching tree decorations (opposite), these presents from nature enhance your home with a feeling of timeless simplicity.

1. LIGHT THE WAY

Not only are these items pretty in their unrefined way, but they give off aromas that many of us associate with happy holiday memories. Set a small votive candle in a glass container (Matthew chose one of his favorite vintage jelly jars; reproductions are available at MatthewMeadCollection. com), and tuck fresh cranberries around it. The warmth from the candle will encourage some of the berry fragrance. Nearby, a sprig of bay leaves also has a crisp scent. Sprinkle clippings or the individual leaves between candles down the center of the table for an irresistible combination. And remember, never leave a burning candle unattended; burnt cranberries don't smell nearly as good as gently warmed ones.

2. HANGING AROUND

These rustic wreaths capture the appeal of a nature walk and are easy to make. For the pinecone circles, cut wreath forms out of cardboard. These measure 5 and 7 inches in diameter. Wrap the cardboard in brown ribbon and secure the ends with hot glue. Rub the tines off several pinecones, then use hot glue to attach then in overlapping layers to cover the ribbon. When finished and dry, make the tines shine with a dusting of gold embossing powder. For the twig wreath, wrap brown twine around the junctions of four pairs of straight, fresh cut branches. You can also purchase similar wreaths already made from crafts stores. Adorn the wreath with a cluster of dried embellishment, such as whole star anise, allspice berries, and other floral supplies from the craft store.

3. MIXED MEDLEY

Stir up your own batch of potpourri to use around the house or to give away. In a large mixing bowl, combine a variety of scented and natural ingredients. We used things we picked up on a walk, such as small pinecones, acorns, and horse chestnuts. Then we embellished the mix with purchased ingredients, including almonds and pecans in their shells, fresh bay leaves, whole star anise, cinnamon sticks, rose hips, and birch bark curls. When you have about 8 cups of ingredients in the bowl, stir in ½ cup of orris root powder, which we bought from an online spice store. It has a faint violet scent and is often used as a preservative in potpourri. We also stirred in 2 ounces of bayberry oil, but you can choose any essential oil you find appealing.

4. WEE WREATH

Use the same technique as the larger wall wreaths to fashion this napkin ring. Cut a small circle form from heavy-duty cardboard (Matthew sacrificed an extra box for these projects); this one measures 2½ inches in diameter. Hot-glue small pinecone tines around the circle and add whole star anise to the top. Gold embossing powder adds extra shine. Nestle the ring into a complementary table setting, including a hardy linen napkin, chunky pottery dinnerware, unpolished silver flatware, and a textural table runner. This runner is part of Matthew's collection of antique linens, but a reproduction of it is available for sale at MatthewMeadCollection.com

HUNTING AND GATHERING HELP

You can gather handfuls of acorns, pinecones, and fallen leaves on public land near your home. But if you need large quantities of clean, unblemished materials, it's best to go to a retail source:

Knud Nielsen
(KnudNielsen.com;
800/633-1682)

Nature's Pressed Flowers
(NaturesPressed.com;
800/850-2499)

Attar Herbs and Spices
(www.AttarHerbs.com;
800/541-6900)

1 2

3 4

HAVE A BALL Simple and organic, these eye-catching balls (this page) show off the textures and colors of nature. You can purchase similar novelties at stores that sell home accessories, fabric, and crafts. You can also make them by hot-gluing potpourri ingredients, cording, strings of beads, and wooden berries to the surface of plain foam crafts-store balls. When you have a selection, pile the balls into a galvanized-metal bucket.

RUSTIC VIEW Think inside the box to display some woodland finds (opposite). This flat, wide wreath form in a modern square shape is a friendly surface to adhere bumpy pinecones. Look for similar forms, usually made of twigs, at the crafts store. You can also purchase variety packs of pinecones, or gather different-size specimens during a walk through the woods. Heat up your glue gun and keep the refills coming as you attach enough cones to cover the frame. When finished, tuck dried moss from the garden center or crafts store into any gaps.

"I am so grateful for the gifts Mother Nature sends."
— Matthew

1. PRETTY LITTLE PACKAGES

These small containers are an elegant way to show your gratitude. Tuck a small trinket, gift card, or movie passes inside a vintage cold cream jar, or set up a wee terrarium that brings holiday cheer. For the tabletop garden, arrange reindeer moss, cranberries, and ivy sprigs in a glass compote or lidded candy jar. Another gift idea uses sleek silver tins from the office supply store: Fill them with writing supplies, including a fountain pen, address labels, and stamps. Bind the boxes together with a ribbon, and add a sprig of greenery.

2. NO-SEW STOCKING

With scissors and glue, you can whip up this cheery stocking in any size you like. Download the stocking template from HolidayWithMatthewMead.com, enlarge it to your desired size and trace it twice onto a piece of felt. Join the two stockings, using fabric glue around the edges, then turn it inside out. To make the cuff, color-copy the leaves onto iron-on printer fabric, which is sheets of 8x10-inch fabric designed to work with home printers. (Look for it at crafts and fabric stores.) Print the leaves, cut them out, and iron them onto the stocking, following the manufacturer's directions. Finally, glue on artificial cranberries.

3. FRAME UPS

Create festive and personal ornaments by choosing the elements you want to feature, such as pressed leaves and pretty papers, or computer-printed sayings, carol titles, or quotes. Then have several pairs of inexpensive glass pieces cut at a local hardware store. Ours measure 2½x3½ inches and 4x4 inches. Sandwich the papers between two pieces of glass, and bind the edges with 1-inch-wide copper tape, which you can buy at home centers, crafts stores, and online. As a final touch, affix copper wire hangers with more glue.

LEAF PRESSING

Any kind of tree foliage—from these red maple leaves, to oak, birch, or laurel leaves—can be pressed flat and dried. Simply place them between the pages of an old phone book, and weigh it down with a heavy rock or brick. Check the leaves every few days; it will take about a week for them to dry completely.

"Look deep into nature, and then you will understand everything better."
— *Albert Einstein*

CANDY
PAPER
SCISSORS

Stephanie Nielson and her children draw inspiration from holiday candy to create a spectacular handmade Christmas using an assortment of pretty papers and a tempting array of sweets.

LIFESTYLE PHOTOGRAPHY BY JUSTIN HACKWORTH

ALL STACKED UP
Stephanie Nielson, contributing lifestyle editor for HOLIDAY, created a tree of sweets (OPPOSITE) by stacking cake stands and topping them with a paper tree, made by threading a flat-bottomed skewer through the center of paper flower ornaments of graduated sizes. She and her children filled the stands with yummy cupcakes, cookies, ornaments, and candy cups. See paper ornament directions on page 74.

SMILE!
Claire, 10, shows off the candy wreath she made with her mother. Find directions on page 78.

HAND-CRAFTED HOLIDAY

Make these paper flower ornaments using reversible sheets of scrapbook paper and double-sided tape.

You will need:

    12x12-inch two-sided scrapbook paper
    Paper cutter or rotary cutter and straight edge
    Stapler
    Double-stick tape
    Flower stickers

1. Using a paper cutter, or a rotary cutter and a straight-edge, cut paper into 1-inch strips. You'll need 20 strips for each flower.

2. Stack the strips and staple the center, then fold the stack in half to make a small fan of paper.

3. Place a piece of tape at the end of the first paper strip and bend it in towards the stapled center, pressing to secure.

4. Repeat until every strip is adhered and a circle of flower petals is formed.

5. Affix a flower sticker from a crafts store to the center of the paper flower.

FLOWER-PACKED TREE

Stephanie's family loves a large, fat tree, and they place it near a window to allow daylight to illuminate the glass ornaments. Tucked into the branches, faux euonymus, red berry branches, and amaryllis blossoms are pops of bright color. Directions for the striking tree topper are on page 80.

READY, SET, DECORATE!

The Nielsons' eldest son, Oliver, gathers up the newly crafted ornaments, including large dove stickers from a crafts store, to hang on the tree and to form into festive garlands.

"Inviting our children to help us deck the halls fills them with such excitement." — *Stephanie*

CUT AND PASTE

Three-dimensional paper ornaments are an inexpensive way to decorate your holiday home.

You will need:
- Templates
- Colored paper
- Double-stick tape
- Hole punch
- Clear monofilament line

1. Download the templates from our website, HolidayWithMatthewMead. com, then use a computer to enlarge and print three of each pattern.

2. Cut out each flower or circle shape; fold each shape down its center.

3. Adhere three like shapes together using double-stick tape.

4. Using a hole punch, make a tiny hole at the top of each ornament and thread loops of clear monofilament line.

1   **2**

3

CANDY BY THE POUND

Look no further than your local sweets shop for inspiration for a multitude of festive projects and gifts. **1.** To make this candy wreath, paint a 6-inch wooden wreath form red, and then use crafts glue to stick an assortment of colorful candy to it. Stephanie used a mix of candied almonds, mints, raspberry marshmallows, and cinnamon candies. Attach a small picture hanger to the back and hang securely from a door or wall. **2.** Cellophane bags filled with candy become fun place cards or party favors when personalized with folded paper cardstock and alphabet stickers; staple along the cards to secure. **3.** Stephanie and the children fill clear glass or plastic ball ornaments (from a crafts store) with candy and use a ribbon to hang the fun decorations on their tree. **4.** Miniature cupcakes, covered in a thick layer of creamy white frosting, are sprinkled with crushed, striped peppermints. Decadent chocolate cookies (see recipe page 136) are nestled in cheery red muffin cups and studded with assorted red candies.

STARBURST TOPIARIES AND TREE TOPPERS

"These trees look great lining a mantle or along your dining table," Stephanie says. Follow steps 1 – 7 to make the tree topper shown on page 75. Download the pattern from HolidayWithMatthewMead.com.

You will need:

- Circle templates (available on our website: HolidayWithMatthewMead.com
- Paper
- Ruler
- Hot glue
- Hot glue sticks
- Wide rubber band, cut into two 1-inch pieces
- Needle and thread

1. Using our template as a guide, trace and cut out ten paper circles.

2. For each circle, use a ruler and pencil to divide it into eight equilateral triangles, and then cut along the lines toward the middle, stopping half an inch from the center of each circle.

3. Wrap each "triangle" around the pencil, starting with a long side, to curl it into a cone, and secure with a dab of hot glue. Repeat for remaining circles until you have 10 star shapes.

4. Poke the needle and thread (knotted at the end), through the center of one of the rubber band pieces. Push the needle through the center points of five of the completed stars with their flat sides facing down. Turn over the remaining five stars, flat sides facing up, and thread them on, followed by the second piece of rubber band.

5. With the pencil, apply pressure to the rubber band to compress the stars into a ball and pull up on the string with your other hand to join the rubber pieces. Adjust the paper cones as needed to make the full three-dimensional starburst.

To make the topiaries:

6. Guide a white-painted dowel through the center of two ornaments, and secure as necessary with hot glue.

7. Press dowel into a painted flowerpot filled with floral foam.

8. Cover foam with small red candies.

"I love the idea of filling a hard-working, colorful tote with tree-trimming supplies"

— Stephanie, NieNieDialogues.blogspot.com

1

2

3

4

CANDY STATION

Create a festive display at one end of a room or along a wide hallway by stacking colorful benches and arranging jars of Christmas candy, collectibles, holiday treat bags, and handmade holiday décor on each level.

1. To make this simple wall tree (opposite) cut 80 circles out of patterned scrapbook paper using a 2-inch circle punch. Arrange the circles and adhere using temporary glue dots (Zots™). Set a cylindrical vase filled with tiny Christmas ornaments below the tree and hang the candy wreath (instructions on page 78) as a topper. **2.** Stephanie loves the innocent appeal of snowmen and created this 3-foot-tall paper version using a variety of 12x12-inch scrapbook papers and heavy white paper. Trace a set of graduated bowls onto both the patterned and white papers. Use double-stick tape to adhere the circles together. Use wide-tip markers to draw on the snowman's face and buttons. Attach to a wall or door using Zots™. **3.** The Nielson children, including Oliver, 6, and Jane, 8, love it when their parents engage them in craft projects, especially during the holidays. **4.** Stephanie found these snowmen picks at a crafts store and tucks them into potted plants, flower arrangements, or uses them as gift toppers.

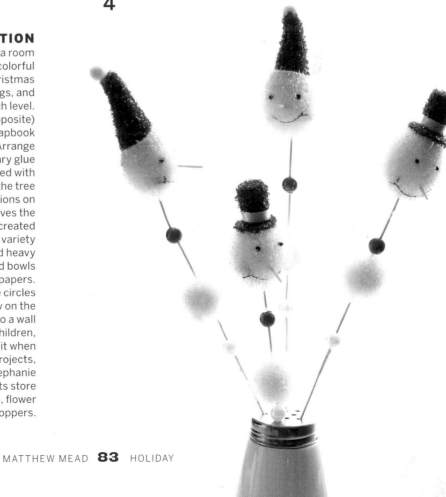

ALL BOXED UP

The faded colors and muted tones of well-loved ornaments and timeworn fabrics recall the charm of Christmases gone by. Look to vintage collectibles and distressed furniture to create an unforgettable holiday scene. Recycled floral boxes can be used to package gifts like handmade ornaments and vintage tea cups — with no gift wrap needed. Simply finish with an organza ribbon and top with a tiny holiday ornament.

TIMEWORN TIDINGS

Add a vintage patina to your holiday decorating with faded florals, soft pastels, and simple projects that stand the test of time.

PAPER ROSES WREATH
Pastel tissue-paper flowers form a dazzling wreath.

You will need:

- 6x6-inch tissue paper squares in pastel hues
- Floral wire
- Hot glue gun
- Hot glue sticks
- 12-inch foam wreath form
- Mercury balls

1. To make flowers, accordion-fold five layers of tissue. Wrap floral wire around the middle of the folded tissue and secure. Create petals by snipping each end of the folds in a pointed or rounded shape. Fan out the folds on one side, up towards the middle; repeat for the other side. Separate and fluff the layers to form a flower shape. Make about 30 flowers.

2. Hot-glue the flowers to cover the wreath form.

3. Attach tiny mercury balls with additional floral wire.

TRIM THE TREE Vintage glass ornaments and paper fans dress a white tree (THIS PAGE). To make a fan, use a 12x12-inch piece of scrapbook paper and make ½-inch wide accordion folds. Once entirely pleated, fold in half and tape together using double-sided tape, then fan out the pleats. For smaller fans, use smaller sheets of scrapbook paper. For interest, layer small fans on top of large ones and adhere using hot glue. Nestle the fans in the tree branches.

HUNG WITH CARE Retro glass balls and faux birds (OPPOSITE) are hallmarks of vintage holiday style. Pastel tissue-paper flowers add soft color, and balance the bold hues of the glass balls.

COLORFUL COLLECTIONS Dig through your grandmother's attic or scour flea markets for vintage decorations. **1.** Collect glass ornaments in your favorite colors and bring back the memories of childhood holidays. **2.** Create quiet impact by focusing your tree décor on a theme. Here, we chose a nostalgic mix of vintage and shiny — unified by a palette of pink, peach, and blue. **3.** Place leftover ornaments on a scalloped antique platter. We made the sparkly bird's nest using a short length of silvery tinsel. **4.** Make an accordion-pleated tree skirt using pretty patterned gift wrap. To make, follow the fan directions on page 86.

OLD-FASHIONED FAVORS Small glass bottles, filled with pearlescent gum balls, are a delightful take-home treat. Wrap tinsel around the neck of each bottle and tie on a miniature vintage mercury glass ornament.

IN BLOOM Fill several large glass jars with water and add in small bouquets of lush pink and orange roses (OPPOSITE) for a breathtaking and unexpected holiday centerpiece. Set into a large wire mesh basket for easy portability throughout your home, or use bouquets for sweet last-minute gifts when friends or neighbors pop in for an unexpected holiday visit.

QUICK IDEAS 1. Break with tradition and fill a pillowcase with small gifts and finish with a pretty ribbon. **2.** Purchase a floral-patterned rectangular box at your local craft store. Enhance the design using colored pencils. **3.** Age an inexpensive journal from a bargain shop by white-washing the cover. Apply white stain with a paint brush and let set for one minute. Wipe off excess stain until desired effect is achieved. Tie a ribbon around the journal and embellish with a pretty pencil and a small ornament. **4.** Decorate gifts with sugar-paste flowers purchased from your local crafts or baking-supply store.

WALL SACHETS
Cover plain hanging sachets with
scrapbook paper, trims, and stickers.

CELEBRATE

Set the table—guests are headed your way!
Wave the neighbors over, call up the family, and send
a few email invites to friends you're longing to
catch up with. This is a season for sharing,
whether it's as little as a cup of coffee, or as special
as a Christmas morning breakfast. Peruse these party
ideas, make a grocery list, and get busy tinkering
in the kitchen or stirring up drinks at the bar.
Go easy on yourself and shop your favorite food stores,
then present their treats in stylish ways.
The secret to holiday entertaining: If you have fun,
your guests will, too.

SUNRISE BREAKFAST

Inside her elegant Brooklyn limestone home, Stefanie Schiada hosts family and friends for a hearty Christmas breakfast — perfect nourishment for a day filled to the brim with festivity.

FESTIVE FINERY AND FOOD

Rising early on Christmas morning is a natural reaction to such an exciting holiday. When hosting a breakfast gathering, plan your menu to include easy-to-prepare foods and keep the details elegant but simple. Stefanie layers her table with sheer silver fabric and lights candles and votives to reflect the sparkle of her favorite crystal and help illuminate a cold winter's morn. White dishes await waffles topped with fresh fruit and cream. OPPOSITE: Known for her attention to detail, Stefanie wrapped plain white napkin rings with birch paper and secured the ends with double-sided tape. You can download the patterned paper, as well as the napkin rings, at HolidayWithMatthewMead.com.

Christmas morning starts early for Luke and Stefanie Schiada — fondly known as Mr. and Mrs Limestone by readers of her popular blog, BrooklynLimestone.com. Nestled on a quiet street, their century-old home — whose loving restoration is chronicled on the blog — greets guests eager to tuck into a breakfast of holiday comfort food. Stefanie confesses that the gathering combines two of her favorite things: designing and creating one-of-a-kind printed holiday menus, place cards, and gift tags — and entertaining. After long hours at her corporate day job, Stefanie feeds her creative spirit by flexing her entertaining chops and by spending some evenings devoted to her graphic design business (SonicStefDesign.com), known for what she calls "unexpected pieces for correspondence." She herself is a client: Says Stefanie, "In place of traditional Christmas cards, I design and create a little gift to send out to family and friends with our season's greetings. From custom-printed dishtowels to bookplates, I love the challenge of coming up with something new each year. It's how I always start my holiday engines." And the Schiadas' home is where friends love to gather. "Our renovation was a labor of love that resulted in a home that is perfect for us," says Stefanie, "and to be able to share Christmas morning here with those special to me is a holiday gift itself."

EAT, DRINK, AND BE MERRY THIS PAGE: Stephanie welcomes guests with a smile. A tray of glassware awaits filling: Skewer fresh berries with hand-crafted drink stirrers to make glasses of orange juice special. OPPOSITE: Stephanie was inspired to create a table menu after spotting rustic birch discs at the flower market. She designed and printed the menu on her computer and transferred the image to the birch disc using t-shirt transfers and a hot iron. Find drink stirrer and wood menu directions on page 137.

SOPHISTICATED HOLIDAY STYLE

THIS PAGE: A sideboard painted in Martha Stewart's Plumage offers display space for decorations, drinks, and a collection of antique silver candlesticks. Stefanie placed a mini Alberta Spruce, its base wrapped in sheer silver fabric, in front of a window for impact and trimmed it with mercury ornaments. OPPOSITE: A glass vase holds branches, silver ornaments, beads, and glittered foliage. Paper star ornament directions can be found on page 137.

ALL THROUGH THE HOUSE **1.** A birch planter holds fresh greens and birch paper pinwheel and star ornaments (see directions on page 137). **2.** The hall tree, original to the home, holds a birch cone filled with flowers and is the perfect spot for floral touches and gifts for guests. **3.** The kitchen island is a casual and easy place to arrange food buffet-style for easy replenishing. **4.** Tin boxes are filled with thoughtful food gifts from Stefanie's kitchen and the festive gift tags are her own design (visit HolidayWithMatthewMead.com for the downloadable pattern).

"I find Christmas morning so magical, and who doesn't just love breakfast foods?"
— *Stefanie Schiada*

O TANNENBAUM After years of dragging a real tree home through the streets of their Brooklyn, New York, neighborhood, the Schiadas switched to a large, lush faux variety, but missed the natural scent. They solved their dilemma by showcasing a small, natural tree prominently on a vintage pedestal table. They decorated it with simple glass balls and paper ornaments (see directions on page 137), and its open location allows them to enjoy its festive fragrance without impeding traffic flow from room to room.

QUICK AND TASTY 1. Make our tropical fruit salad or buy it ready-made from your grocer's deli. **2.** Pre-made Belgian waffles can be found in the bakery department of the grocery store. Heat gently in the oven and serve with fresh raspberries and whipped cream. **3.** Beignets, served with coffee and raspberry mimosas, are a perfect breakfast finger food. **4.** Make your own cinnamon buns or purchase a bake-and-serve variety and dress them up with orange cream cheese glaze (recipe below) and Christmas trees cut from orange peel. See page 136 for fruit salad and mimosa recipes.

ORANGE CREAM CHEESE GLAZE

You will need:

    2 cups cream cheese, at room temperature

    1 cup powdered sugar, sifted

    1/3 cup milk

    4 tablespoons fresh, grated orange zest
    (reserve two tablespoons for garnish)

1. In a medium bowl, beat the softened cream cheese with a hand mixer on medium speed until smooth.

2. Add the powdered sugar and milk alternately and mix on low speed after each addition until thoroughly mixed.

3. Stir in orange zest.

4. Spread glaze over slightly warmed cinnamon buns and top with remaining orange zest.

ORANGE PEEL CHRISTMAS TREES

To make these fanciful orange Christmas trees, remove the peel from large sections of thick-skinned orange. Using a 2-inch Christmas tree cookie cutter, cut out the festive shapes. Use a paring knife to clean up and sculpt the tree-shaped design. Refrigerate until ready to use.

PENGUIN TREATS

There's nothing formal about this jolly children's party featuring tuxedo-clad cold-weather friends. You can recreate the bold decorations and yummy treats just by visiting a crafts store and our website.

SET THE HAPPY SCENE

Bouquets of bright yellow balloons mark the treat buffet. Hang paper snowflakes and pinwheels from the ceiling, and array wrapped juice drinks, pudding cups, and dishes of candy around the cake. For the drink wraps, download the design at HolidayWithMatthewMead.com. You can find paper snowflakes wherever party supplies are sold.

TASTY TREATS Offer yellow candies, such as M&M's® or gumballs, and individual pudding cups. To make them, fill a clean, small crafts-store bucket with pudding up to ½ inch from the top. Fill the remaining space with whipped cream, and smooth it using a water-moistened spatula. Cut a smaller circle out of parchment paper (we traced the bottom of the bucket) and lay it gently off-center on the whipped cream. Cover the exposed whipped cream with crushed chocolate-cookie crumbs. Remove the paper circle. Make the face using icing eyes, and eyebrows and a beak formed out of ready-made fondant from the crafts store.

MILK PUPPETS For these waddling sippers, use a funnel to fill empty soda or condiment containers with milk. You can reuse clean bottles or purchase new ones from a crafts store or restaurant-supply store. Download the wings template from HolidayWithMatthewMead.com, or turn to page 143, and cut them from black construction paper. Attach them with double-stick tape. Top each bottle with a head made from a chocolate donut hole. Icing eyes and small fondant beaks—materials available at the crafts store—complete the penguin face. Finally, wrap a scarf of mini-ball fringe.

1. PARTY PREP

Have fun embellishing your rooms with decorations and games that fit the theme. These paper balloons are Japanese children's toys we found online; they can be used again and again. At party supply stores, you'll also find penguin piñatas and mylar balloons. While you're there, stock up on cups, plates and napkins that fit the color theme. Choosing colorful polka-dot dinnerware—rather than character-themed paper goods—allows you to re-use them for another event or party.

2. LET THEM EAT CAKE

The centerpiece of your treats table is this dashing penguin cake.

You will need:

- Your favorite cake mix
- 1 container chocolate frosting
- Black icing color, such as Wilton®
- 8-inch round cake stencil
- 8 ounces desiccated coconut
- Icing eyes
- Ready-made fondant in black, yellow, and tan
- Pastry bag tips

1. Bake two 9-inch cakes according to package directions. Let cool.

2. Use concentrated icing color to tint chocolate frosting black. Frost cake layers. To get a smooth, shiny surface, dip your metal spatula in warm water as you smooth the frosting.

3. Place the cake stencil on the cake, slightly off center, and fill the area with desiccated coconut (dried, finely flaked coconut from the baking aisle of the grocery store).

4. Add icing eyes and fondant decorations. To make the polka dots for the bow tie, roll out yellow fondant and punch circles using pastry bag tips.

3. HOME PLATE

No need to invest in specialty dinnerware for the party. Just personalize a plain plate by layering our cute paper penguin face on top of the plate and under a smaller glass salad plate. Download the inserts from HolidayWithMatthewMead.com.

4. FROSTY BIRDS

Make your own push pops by purchasing the plastic containers that you can fill with any blend of frozen confection.

You will need:

- Banana, chocolate, and white chocolate puddings
- Black food coloring
- Push pop containers (from an online specialty food store)
- Black paper
- Double-stick tape
- Penguin stickers

1. Tint the chocolate pudding black using food coloring.

2. Layer banana, black-tinted chocolate, and white chocolate pudding in containers.

3. Wrap bands of black paper around the containers and affix with double-stick tape.

4. Freeze overnight. Just before the party, add penguin stickers.

ENTERTAINMENT PICKS

GAMES Play "Pin the Beak on the Penguin" using a wildlife poster from a museum or zoo shop, or make your own using black markers, white poster board, and orange construction paper beaks. Other timeless favorites, such as Musical Chairs, can be updated with a penguin theme. Ask the kids to waddle around the circle until they find seats. Or, play the variation: Duck, Duck, Penguin!

MOVIES In the background of the festivities, show *March of the Penguins* (rated G, 2005), *Happy Feet* (rated PG, 2006), or *Mr. Popper's Penguins* (rated PG, 2011).

MUSIC Soundtracks for the movies mentioned above make great background tunes, and songs can be stopped and started for a rousing rendition of Musical Chairs. Look also for the soundtrack for the movie *Happy Feet Two in 3D.*

1

2

3

4

THE COMPLETE PACKAGE Guests won't be able to resist these welcoming invitations (ABOVE, LEFT). Download them from HolidayWithMatthewMead.com and print them on cardstock. Punch two holes for threading the ball-fringe scarf, and a hole at the top for a garnish of twine.

CUTE SIPPERS For these juice drink wraps (ABOVE, RIGHT), we've done the work for you. Visit our website and download the pre-sized designs. You can even add the names from your guest list using Adobe® Photoshop®. Not sure who's coming yet? Copy the wraps from page 143, then rub on letter decals from the crafts store at the last minute.

TAKE-AWAY GIFTS
As the party winds down,
stack up a variety of empty
gift boxes and invite guests
to fill them with their choice
of take-home treats, such as
desserts, candy, balloons,
and snowflake decorations.

FESTIVAL OF LIGHTS

Hanukkah is a Jewish celebration that lasts eight days and nights. Rich with symbolism, it is a time for friends and family to gather together to light the menorah, enjoy customary foods, and celebrate its traditions.

WAYS WITH LIGHT

Blue, silver, and white make up the usual color palette associated with Hanukkah. Add in shades of lavender for an unexpected twist. The miracle of light has deep significance during Hanukkah. Light your celebration with pretty votive holders made with lavender hued drinking glasses and cake-decorating store dragées.

GIFT EXCHANGE
Although the only traditional Hanukkah gift is "gelt" (small amounts of money), small, meaningful gifts are sometimes exchanged. Here, elegantly wrapped gifts are nestled in a large basket for children to enjoy following the meal. A variation on the menorah, nine candle tapers — anchored in kosher salt — await lighting.

MODERN PAPER ORNAMENTS

Use paper in complementary colors to make these graphic holiday ornaments.

You will need:

- Cutting mat
- Cardstock or scrapbook paper
- Utility knife
- Metal ruler
- Stapler
- Clear monofilament line

1. Working on a cutting mat, use the utility knife and a ruler to cut paper into seven 1x11-inch strips.

2. Choose colors for each ornament (we used two colors per ornament).

3. Cut a 6-inch center strip and pairs of strips in 7-, 9-, and 11-inch lengths respectively, to form each of the three concentric layers. Strips can be made longer or shorter depending on the overall ornament size desired.

4. Place the 6-inch center strip in the middle of the other layers. Line up the top edges and staple to secure.

5. Line up the bottom edges of the strips and staple. Next, press the strips together 2 inches from the top edge and staple to create the final shape.

6. To hang, slip some clear monofilament line through the top loop of each ornament.

BREAKING BREAD

Fried foods, like latkes (potato pancakes), are eaten during Hanukkah to honor the miracle of the oil. Dipped in applesauce, the crispy pancakes are a highlight of the meal. Traditional braided challah bread is dense and slightly sweet, and its pull-apart hunks are most delicious when warm from the oven and brushed with butter. Surprise your guests with small packages — wrapped in embossed paper and bearing chocolate coins — as a reminder to engage in charity and good deeds throughout the year.

GLASS MENORAH TRIVET

A menorah is lit for the eight days of Hanukkah to commemorate the miracle of the oil. Once lit, it is placed in front of a window. We applied a paper image of the revered holiday symbol under a glass trivet, for a purposeful holiday display.

You will need:

    Menorah template, available as a download on our website

    One glass trivet or candle base, from a craft supplies store.

    Small sponge paintbrush

    Mod Podge®

1. Download and print the menorah template on white paper.

2. Cut the paper to fit the dimensions of the glass trivet or candle base.

3. Use a sponge brush to apply Mod Podge® to the underside of the glass.

4. Carefully set the menorah image in place. Let dry.

FESTIVE-WRAPPED HANUKKAH PACKAGES

During the much-anticipated holiday, children are often gifted with one special present per day.

You will need:

    An assortment of colorful plain and patterned wrapping paper in shades of blue, lilac, silver, and gold

    Clear adhesive tape

    Several lengths of #40 ribbon

    Glue gun

    Hot glue sticks

    Several lengths of satin and sheer French wire ribbon

1. Carefully wrap packages using assorted papers and adhesive tape.

2. Wrap each gift with ribbons of your choice and secure with hot glue on underside of packages.

3. For a layered effect, overlap ribbons and add bows made using French wire ribbon.

MINIATURE POPPY SEED MUFFINS

Poppy seeds and lemon come together in one scrumptiously moist muffin. (See glaze recipe, at right)

You will need:

    2 cups all-purpose flour

    ¾ cup sugar

    1 teaspoon each baking soda and baking powder

    ¼ teaspoon salt

    2 eggs

    1 cup sour cream

    ½ cup vegetable oil

    2 Tablespoons milk

    2 Tablespoons poppy seeds

    ½ teaspoon each lemon extract and pure vanilla extract

1. Preheat oven to 400 degrees; grease or line mini-muffin pan.

2. In a large bowl, blend flour sugar, baking soda, baking powder, and salt.

3. In a separate bowl, combine eggs, sour cream, oil, milk, poppy seeds, and lemon and vanilla extracts.

4. Mix well and add to dry ingredients, stirring until just moistened.

5. Pour batter into muffin cups until two-thirds full and bake 8 – 10 minutes or until cake tester comes out clean.

VANILLA GLAZE

Pour over muffins or cupcakes for a sweet finish. Top with colored sugars and Star of David template from HolidayWithMatthewMead.com.

You will need:

    2 cups sifted confectioner's sugar

    1½ Tablespoons softened butter

    ½ teaspoon pure vanilla extract

    ¼ teaspoon salt

    4 to 5 Tablespoons milk

    A variety of colored sugars

1. Combine ingredients in small mixing bowl, adding more milk if needed.

2. Stir until smooth and well blended, adding milk if needed.

3. Spread icing or drizzle over warm muffins or cupcakes.

4. Sprinkle cooled glazed muffins or cupcakes with colored sugar. For a Hanukkah-themed dessert, set the stencil atop the glazed cupcakes. Lightly dust with the colored sugar, then carefully remove stencil.

1 2

3 4

DECKED OUT Create your own traditional décor: **1.** Make a Star of David wreath by bending two 28-gauge floral wire strands (14-inch lengths) into two equilateral triangles. Wrap both triangles in florist's tape. Invert one and wire it to the top of the other using 24-gauge floral wire. Cut snippets of greenery and wire to the wreath; it will remain fresh throughout Hanukkah. **2.** A dreidel gift tag is made using air-dry clay, a cookie cutter, and some glitter glue. **3.** A purchased birdhouse from Michael's resembles the iconic dreidel. Basecoat it in white and create a square pattern with a checkerboard stencil and lavender and blue paint. **4.** Have a craftsperson build a 3-foot-wide Star of David out of a wooden frame. Wire on greenery and hang over a mantel or above an exterior door to announce the holiday.

TRADITION REIGNS

Use fabrics and decorative papers — in classic Hanukkah colors — to dress up your holiday home. Add simple flourishes by layering furniture with beautiful pillows and elegant linens. Add sparkle with candlelight, and round out your celebration with fresh flowers and greenery tucked into julep cups. Wrap small gifts in textured papers and festoon with colorful bows. Then, throw open your doors and welcome family and friends in to celebrate the significance of the holiday.

SENSATIONAL NEW YEAR

With some simple changes and colorful updates, your holiday décor will see you into the New Year with style. Follow along as DIY queen Kate Riley shows you how to celebrate BIG on a modest budget.

USHER IN THE NEW YEAR THIS PAGE: Silver trays rest on tables and shelves throughout the main entertaining spaces of Kate's San Francisco Bay area home. Topped with champagne flutes and party horns — ready for the moment the clock strikes twelve — they are in easy reach of guests. To make your own colorful noisemakers, purchase horns at a party supply store and cover in patterned scrapbook paper and affix with double-stick tape. OPPOSITE: Fill your best bowls and platters with shiny pink and green ornaments, chartreuse greenery, and sparkling Mardi Gras beads to create instant glamorous centerpieces for your home.

COLORFUL NEW YEAR **1.** Inexpensive glass ornaments can be found after Christmas at a deep discount. Purchase bold colored ones to add impact to your décor. **2.** A sparkly twig tree anchors Kate's dessert buffet. Resting on a table covered in stiff drapery lining, it is decorated with shapely pink ornaments and illuminated by the fading daylight. **3.** A length of lace ribbon dresses up a glass compote filled with Mexican Wedding cookies. **4.** Kate swirled pink acrylic paint inside this glass ornament and embellished it with a light dusting of ice glitter and a foil snowflake sticker.

CELEBRATE WITH A TOAST

Miniature pink millimeter mercury balls are wired to champagne flutes for easy and impactful celebratory style. Keep the champagne flowing by placing ice buckets filled with well-chilled bottles in every room. Keep a bowlful of small delicate cookies (like these store-bought Mexican Wedding cookies) nearby to nibble on between sips.

1

2

3

Quick and stylish ideas keep Kate's home fresh and celebratory.
Readers of her blog CentsationalGirl.com love Kate for her savvy and
thoughtful approach to affordable design.

4

PRETTY DETAILS

1. Dress up chairs with green damask table runners. **2.** Drizzle chocolate wafer cookies with warmed strawberry frosting. **3.** Kate loves the easier pace that follows Christmas and relies on foolproof entertaining ideas. **4.** Kate's friend Kathleen raises her glass in a toast. **5.** Cookie cutters brushed with glue and sprinkled with glass glitter reflect the sparkle of the celebration. **6.** Boxed desserts — wrapped in lace trim and topped with printable labels—are elegant take-home party favors. **7.** Ornaments spill forth from a bowl and can be easily slipped into storage on January 2nd. **8.** A printed fabric-transfer pillow, filled with lavender from Kate's garden, has a special message for 2012. Print the design onto fabric (download the pattern at HolidayWithMatthewMead.com) and stitch together. Finish with a cutting of linen ribbon to hang.

5

6

7

8

EDIBLE GARNISH
Store-bought meringue cookies hang from satin ribbons for unique tree ornaments.

EXCITEMENT IN THE AIR Falling just six days after Christmas, New Year's Eve promises one more exciting celebration before bidding adieu to December. **1.** Ever imaginative, Kate uses a large clear glass vase in lieu of an ice bucket and adds sparkle with a string of colorful beads. **2.** Set the stage for your New Year's bash by adding fresh color to the mix and rearranging holiday décor, like Kate did with the wintery vignette on this curved sideboard. **3.** Colorful paper napkins offer graphic appeal. **4.** Kate's five-year-old son grins over a stack of candy canes — leftovers from the family Christmas tree.

HELP YOURSELF
The dining room is set for dessert and the doors of this hard-working built-in cabinet are kept open to show off Kate's holiday collections and to offer easy access to coffee cups for those guests who enjoy java with a generous slice of chocolate cheesecake.

ENDURING TRADITIONS Kate loves to use fresh greenery for its nostalgic Christmas scent. Whether purchased or clipped from her backyard, it is a budget-friendly way to bring nature indoors. As the holiday season nears its end, Kate gives the fresh greenery a boost by tucking faux sprigs into garlands and wreaths. ABOVE: A cedar garland is draped along the mantel and lit candles reflect in the mirror. (Cedar garland: LynchCreekWreaths.com) BELOW: Kate prefers to spend time with guests, and thus chooses her party menu wisely. OPPOSITE: Fill apothecary jars with favorite vintage ornaments.

"The best moments of the holiday season happen when we spend time with the ones we love, so don't be afraid to entertain."
— *Kate Riley*

1   2
3   4

SWEET SENSATION Avoid endless hours of baking by visiting your local bakery for fresh pastries, tarts, and cakes. **1.** Kate's holiday dishware, with its simple snowflake detail, can be used throughout winter. **2.** She looked to her grocer for chocolate-covered pretzels and English toffee dipped in chocolate and nuts. **3.** Round out the sweet buffet with Christmas candy and chocolates. **4.** Kate embellished miniature cheesecakes by melting strawberry frosting and white chocolate, then drizzling it on top. To make, simply microwave a tub of frosting (or white chocolate pieces) on medium heat for 30 seconds, or until thin.

GROUP EFFORT The highlight of the dessert buffet is this cheesecake Kate bought at her favorite bakery and garnished with boxed chocolates. "My dessert buffet is incomplete without the three C's: chocolate, cheesecake, and champagne!" Kate says with a laugh. And after a busy festive season, she happily accepts offers from guests to bring along their signature holiday desserts or small bites to share.

recipes

HOLIDAY COOKIES

GINGER COOKIES WITH ROYAL ICING

This recipe is adapted from Around My French Table *by Dorie Greenspan (Houghton Mifflin Harcourt; 2010)*

You will need:

- 7 Tablespoons salted butter, softened
- ½ cup granulated sugar
- ½ cup brown sugar
- 1 large egg
- 1 ⅔ cup flour
- ¼ teaspoon salt
- ¼ teaspoon baking soda
- 2 teaspoons cinnamon
- ½ teaspoon ground ginger
- ¼ teaspoon ground cloves

1. Preheat the oven to 350 degrees.

2. In a stand mixer, cream the butter with the sugars until fluffy.

3. Add the egg and beat, then add the flour, salt, baking soda, and spices in three batches, beating between each addition until just combined.

4. Divide the dough into two. Form each piece of dough into a flat disk and chill until firm.

5. Roll out each disk of dough to about ¼-inch thickness, and use a cookie cutter to cut out. Transfer the cut out cookies to a cookie sheet lined with a silicone mat, and bake for 10 minutes. Cool on a wire rack before decorating.

For the royal icing, you will need:

- 4 Tablespoons meringue powder
- ½ cup water
- 1 pound confectioner's sugar
- 1 teaspoon light corn syrup

1. Combine the meringue powder and water in the bowl of a stand mixer. Using the paddle attachment, beat until foamy. Switch to low speed and sift in the sugar. Mix to combine. Add the corn syrup and beat on high speed for about 5 minutes until stiff peaks form.

2. Put the stiff icing into an icing bag fitted with a plain round #3 tip. (You can also put icing into a sealable plastic bag and snip off a small piece of a corner.) Pipe the designs on each cookie.

FIVE-SPICE SNAILS

A combination of cinnamon, anise seed, star anise, ginger, and clove, Chinese 5-spice powder emits a tantalizing aroma while these cookies bake.

You will need:

- ½ cup granulated sugar
- 2 teaspoons Chinese 5-spice powder
- 1 sheet frozen puff pastry, thawed

1. Preheat the oven to 350 degrees.

2. Sprinkle your work surface with sugar and a little 5-spice. Lay the thawed pastry on the work surface, sprinkle with 5-spice and sugar, and fold lengthwise into thirds. Sprinkle the pastry with more sugar and 5-spice and roll out into a thin rectangle, about 13X15 inches, pressing the 5-spice and sugar into the dough. Sprinkle more sugar and 5-spice over the dough, then roll up into a log starting on the long side. Wrap the spiral in plastic wrap and chill at least 30 minutes.

3. Slice the log into ½-inch slices and arrange on a cookie sheet lined with parchment paper. Bake 13 – 15 minutes, or until crisp and the pastry is baked through.

BOURBON BALLS

These are Kate's grandmother's famous recipe, and they don't require a bit of baking.

You will need:

- 10 ounces graham crackers, crushed into fine crumbs
- 1 cup walnut halves, ground finely in a food processor
- ½ cup confectioner's sugar
- 6 ounces semisweet chocolate chips

½ cup bourbon

3 Tablespoons golden syrup or light corn syrup

Extra granulated sugar or decorative sanding sugar

1. Combine the graham cracker crumbs, ground walnuts, and confectioner's sugar in a large mixing bowl.

2. In a glass bowl, heat the chocolate chips for 30 seconds, then in 10 second intervals, stirring between each interval, until the chips are mostly melted. They'll melt as you stir. Add in bourbon and corn syrup and stir to combine (the chocolate will seize a bit, and the bourbon won't incorporate well. Just do the best you can).

3. Add the chocolate mixture to the crumbs mixture, and stir until thoroughly combined. Chill at least 30 minutes.

4. Pour granulated sugar or decorative sanding sugar into a dish. Form the chocolate mixture into small balls the size of grapes, and roll each ball in the sugar. Store for up to a month in a lidded container.

ALMOND FINANCIERS

This recipe, adapted from DorieGreenspan.com, uses almond flour, which gives the cakelike cookies a rich, nutty flavor.

You will need:

12 Tablespoons salted butter

1 cup sugar

1 cup almond flour

6 egg whites

⅔ cup flour

1. Preheat oven to 400 degrees.

2. In a small saucepan, heat the butter over medium-low heat until it gives off a nutty aroma and is a deep golden brown color. Let cool.

3. Combine the sugar, almond flour, and egg whites in a saucepan. Heat over low heat, stirring constantly, until the mixture is pale, runny and hot. Blend in the flour and the browned butter, which will not want to incorporate but will, after much stirring. Chill the batter until cold. It will be quite firm.

4. Grease the financier molds or mini-muffin tins with a butter-flour spray, or butter and flour each mold. Fill each mold just to the top with batter and scrape out any excess.

5. Bake for 13 minutes, or until the tops are crisp and browned. Remove from the molds and cool.

CHOCOLATE PEPPERMINT TIFFIN

This recipe of Kate's was featured on HolidayWithMatthewMead.com.

You will need:

3 ounces peppermint candy, crushed

15 ounces condensed milk

9 ounces chopped semisweet chocolate

7 ounces butter

7 ounces digestive biscuits (Carr's Whole Wheat crackers or McVitie's Digestive Biscuits)

1 ounce peppermint candy

1. Butter a 10x6-inch pan. Set aside.

2. In a small saucepan, combine the crushed peppermint candy with the condensed milk and heat over low heat, stirring frequently, until the candy has melted.

3. Melt the chocolate and the butter together in a large glass bowl by heating for 30 seconds, then in additional 10 second intervals, stirring between each interval, until the chocolate is melted and the mixture is smooth.

4. Crush the digestive biscuits into large chunks and combine them with the chocolate. Spread half the digestive biscuit mixture into the prepared pan, and freeze for 5 – 10 minutes, or until firm.

5. Pour the condensed milk mixture over the chocolate mixture in the pan, and return to the freezer for another 5 – 10 minutes.

6. Crush the remaining 1 ounce of peppermint candy and stir into the remaining digestive biscuit mixture. Spread the over the peppermint filling, and chill until firm. Cut into small squares and refrigerate until served.

CANDY, PAPER, SCISSORS

CANDY-STUDDED CHOCOLATE COOKIES

Low in fat, these dense, chewy cookies will satisfy any chocolate craving.

You will need:

- 1 cup semisweet chocolate chips
- 3 large egg whites, at room temperature
- 2½ cups confectioner's sugar, divided
- ½ cup unsweetened cocoa powder
- 1 Tablespoon cornstarch
- ¼ teaspoon salt
- 2 cups small red candies or candy-coated chocolates

1. Preheat oven to 400°F, and grease two 9x13-inch baking sheets with vegetable spray.

2. In a glass bowl, melt 1 cup of chocolate chips in the microwave, stirring every 30 seconds for about 2 minutes, or until melted. Let cool slightly.

3. Using a stand mixer set on high speed, beat the egg whites until soft peaks form, then slowly add 1 cup confectioner's sugar. Continue beating until mixture resembles soft marshmallow cream.

4. In a medium bowl, whisk together cocoa, cornstarch, salt, and 1 cup confectioner's sugar.

5. Turning the mixer to low speed, gradually add the dry ingredients to the egg mixture. Add the cooled chocolate. At this point, the dough will become very stiff.

6. Place ½ cup confectioner's sugar in a small bowl. Roll 1 rounded tablespoon of dough into a ball; roll in sugar, coating thickly. Place on greased baking sheet.

7. Repeat with remaining dough, spacing balls 2 inches apart. Bake for about 10 minutes, or until the cookies are puffed and their tops crack. Remove from oven and press candy into tops of cookies. Let cool on baking sheets for 10 minutes. Transfer to rack; continue to let cool.

Makes about 24 cookies

SUNRISE BREAKFAST

MORNING TROPICAL SALAD

This tasty and healthy fruit salad will provide a boost of energy for a hectic Christmas day.

You will need:

- 1 large ripe mango, diced
- 3 whole oranges, peeled and cut into sections
- 2 cups fresh pineapple, cubed
- 2 cups cantaloupe, cubed
- 4 kiwi, peeled and cut into quarters
- 2 Tablespoons lemon juice
- 2 teaspoons honey

1. In a medium stainless steel bowl, combine the fruit, lemon juice, and honey. Mix well and cover.

2. Refrigerate for 1 hour before serving to let the flavors blend.

RASPBERRY MIMOSA

Update your tried-and-true mimosa recipe with the addition of fresh raspberries.

You will need:

- ½ cup brandy
- 3 Tablespoons clear raspberry brandy
- 4½ Tablespoons granulated sugar
- 1 cup fresh raspberries, mashed
- Whole fresh raspberries for garnish
- 1 bottle chilled champagne or sparkling white wine

1. In a glass pitcher, stir brandies and sugar in a medium bowl. Add mashed raspberries and let stand 1 hour at room temperature; then strain.

2. Divide brandy mixture among 6 flutes, adding several whole raspberries to each glass.

3. Pour champagne over fruit-brandy mixture and serve.

projects

FUN FESTIVE WRAPPINGS

NEWSPAPER ROSETTES

Use these to embellish packages or gift tags.

You will need:

Newspaper strips

Hot glue gun

Hot glue sticks

1. Tear newspaper into strips. (The thicker the strip, the larger the rose.)

2. Twist the paper and carefully tie a knot at one end.

3. Coil the twisted paper around to create a rose. Glue as needed.

4. Trim the excess paper from the bottom of the rose.

SUNRISE BREAKFAST

PAPER STAR ORNAMENTS

Make these easy and festive paper flowers.

You will need:

Ruler

12x12-inch sheet of birch-bark-pattern paper from HolidayWithMatthewMead.com

Hot glue gun

Hot glue sticks

Faux jewel flower stickers

1. Measure and cut the paper into five strips, each 1¼ x 8½ inches long.

2. Fold each strip in half lengthwise and gently press the fold to make the paper look like a petal.

3. Glue open end of each petal together.

4. Repeat with remaining four strips and glue all pieces (cut end in towards center) together to form a flower shape.

5. Place a sticker on the center of the flower on each side.

DRINK STIRRERS

Turn the Paper Star Ornaments into fun party stirrers..

1. Measure and cut the paper into 3½x1-inch strips.

2. Repeat steps 2 to 5.

3. Glue wooden bamboo skewer between two of the petals.

WOOD MENUS

Go natural with your table décor and rest these unique table menus at each place setting.

You will need:

Circular discs from a birch tree

Sandpaper

Menu template (available at BrooklynLimestone.com)

Transfer paper for a white t-shirt (found at office-supply stores)

Iron

1. Lightly sand the wooden disc to smooth its surface.

2. Print the menu template in reverse on transfer paper.

3. Set your iron to its highest setting (do not use steam), and iron the pattern onto the wood. Press the iron firmly and keep it moving to avoid scorching.

4. Allow a few seconds to cool, then peel away the transfer paper while still hot.

PINWHEEL ORNAMENTS

Nestle pinwheels in a floral arrangement, tuck on top of gifts, or hang from your tree or ceiling.

You will need:

Scoring board

12x12-inch sheet of birch-bark-pattern paper from HolidayWithMatthewMead.com

Hot-glue gun

Hot glue sticks

1. Using a scoring board, make 1-inch score lines along the entire sheet of paper.

2. Follow the lines to make accordion folds from one edge of the sheet to the other.

3. Fold each accordion-folded sheet in half. Pinch the center to hold the shape, and hot-glue along the fold to fuse it together. This will form a "fan" shape that is one half of the medallion.

4. Bring the two ends of the "fan" together and secure with hot glue to complete the circular pinwheel shape.

templates

Snowflake
page 13

Refillable
Snow Globe
page 11

Stocking
page 12

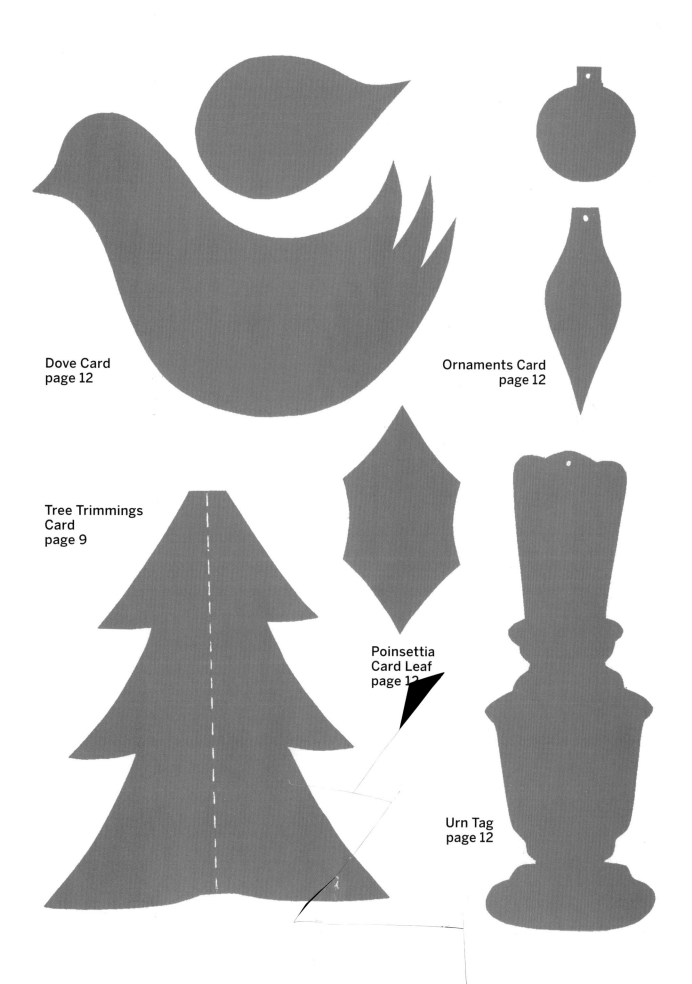

Dove Card
page 12

Ornaments Card
page 12

Tree Trimmings
Card
page 9

Poinsettia
Card Leaf
page 12

Urn Tag
page 12

Glitter Tree Small
page 27

Glitter Tree Large
page 25

Tree of Lights
Candle
page 28

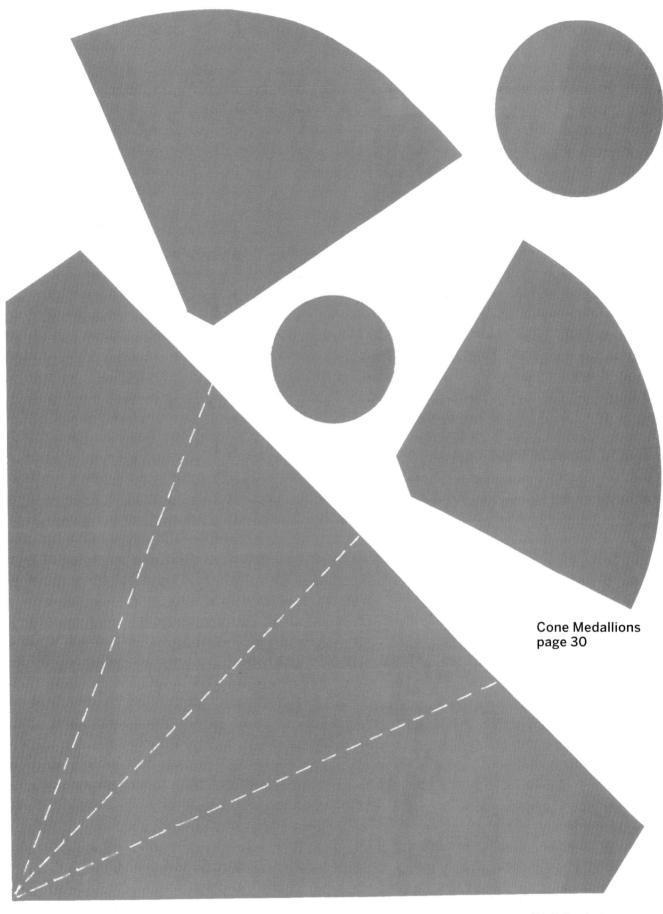

Cone Medallions
page 30

Wall Pocket
page 29

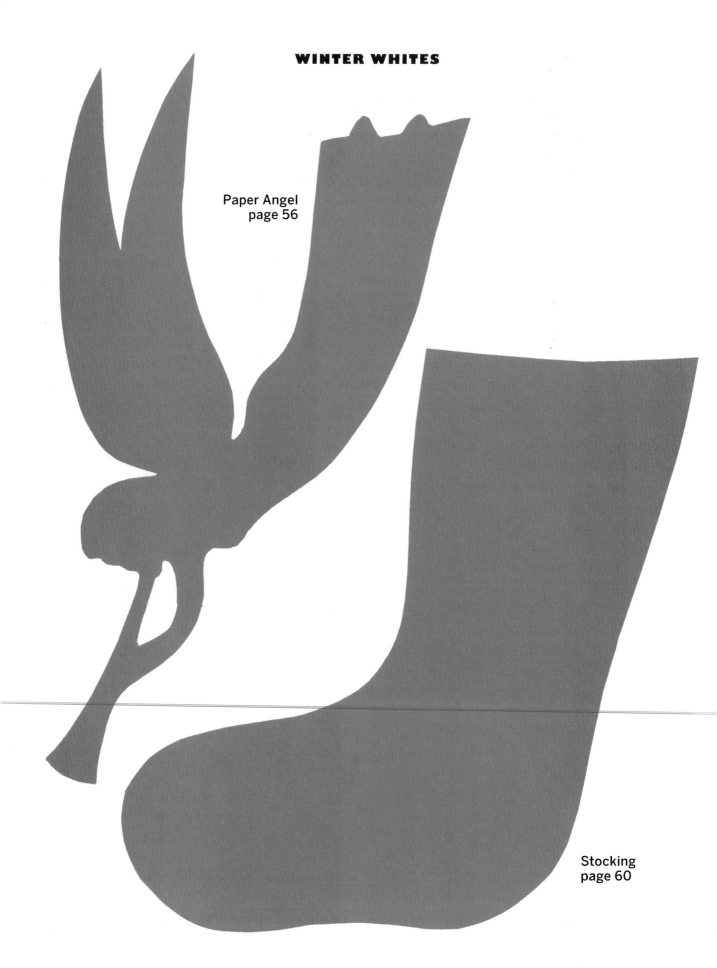

Paper Angel
page 56

Stocking
page 60

Home Plate
page 111

Milk Puppets
page 109

Cute Sippers
page 112

resources

The materials and ingredients for the recipes and projects in this issue of **HOLIDAY** with Matthew Mead can be found at the following retail outlets:

CAKE AND COOKIE DECORATING
The Baker's Kitchen
TheBakersKitchen.net

Chandlers Cake and Candy Supplies
ChandlersCakeandCandy.com

Chef Tools Network, Inc
ChefTools.com

Fancy Flours
FancyFlours.com

Garnish
ThinkGarnish.com/store

Wilton
Wilton.com

CRAFTS
A.C. Moore Arts & Crafts
ACMoore.com

Anything In Stained Glass
AnythingInStainedGlass.com

Create For Less
CreateForLess.com

CrochetGeek
CrochetGeek.com

DIY Bangles
DIYBangles.com

Fiskars
Fiskars.com

JoAnn Fabric and Craft Stores
JoAnn.com

June Tailor, Inc.
JuneTailor.com

Michaels Stores
Michaels.com

Rustic Woodworking
RusticWoodworking.com

Scrapbook online
Scrapbook.com

Snowy Lane Crafts
SnowyLaneCrafts.com

ENTERTAINING
Fish's Eddy
FishsEddy.com

HOME DECOR
Crate & Barrel
CrateAndBarrel.com

IKEA
Ikea.com

Luna Bazaar
LunaBazaar.com

Macy's
Macys.com

Matthew Mead Collection
MatthewMeadCollection.com

Pier 1 Imports
Pier1.com

Target
Target.com

TJX Companies
HomeGoods.com

TJMaxx.com
MarshallsOnline.com

West Elm
WestElm.com

NATURE CRAFTS SUPPLIES
Attar Herbs and Spices
AttarHerbs.com

Knud Nielsen
KnudNielsen.com

Lynch Creek Farm
LynchCreekWreaths.com

Maine Wreath Company
MaineWreathCo.com

Nature's Pressed Flowers
NaturesPressed.com

Seashell World
SeashellWorld.com

OFFICE SUPPLY
The Container Store
ContainerStore.com

Staples
Staples.com

zzzzHolidayWithMatthewMead.com

WRAPPING PAPERS AND PARTY SUPPLIES
Crayola
Crayola.com

Paper Mart
PaperMart.com

Paper Source
Paper-Source.com

Pearl River, Inc.
PearlRiver.com

PIKKU
PIKKUwares.com

Printables By Amy Locurto
PrintablesByAmy.com

Red River Paper
RedRiverCatalog.com

For more information about these projects or recipes, please visit our blogging friends at:

FOOD
Savour-Fare.com

CRAFTS
InspireCo.com
NieNieDialogues.com

DECORATING
BrooklynLimestone.com
CentsationalGirl.com
CheapDecorating.Blogspot.com
HolidayWithMatthewMead.com
ReStyledHome.com